SPICES & SOULS

A DOODLER'S JOURNEY THROUGH KERALA

TEXT AND SKETCHES BY

UNNY

DESIGNED BY ANOOP KAMATH

 **D C Books**

KOTTAYAM - 686 001, KERALA STATE, INDIA

Kerala Editions-1

SPICES & SOULS
A Doodler's Journey Through Kerala
Text and Sketches by E. P. Unny

Right reserved
First Published: July 2001

Design and Layout: Anoop Kamath

Publishers: DC Books, Kottayam - 686 001
Kerala State, India
Website: www.dcbooks.com
e-mail: dcbooks@sancharnet.in
Online Bookstore: www.dcbookstore.com

Distributors: DC Books

Thiruvananthapuram, Kottayam, Thekkady, Kochi, Kalamassery

Nedumbassery (Airport), Kozhikode, New Delhi

Current Books

Thiruvananthapuram, Kollam, Pathanamthitta, Alappuzha,

Kottayam, Thodupuzha, Kochi, Aluva, Irinjalakuda, Palakkad,

Kozhikode, Vatakara, Thalassery, Kalpetta, DC Bookshop

Thrissur, Kairali Pusthakasala Thrissur

ISBN 81-264-0332-2

Printed at: International Print-0-Pac, Ltd.
New Delhi

Price Indian Rs 595.00
US$ 19.95
UK£ 14.95

To

N. Vijayaraghavan

(1945-2000)

Acknowledgements

Abul Kalam Azad, Gautaman Bhaskaran, F.C. Danvers, T. Damu, M.K. Das, Devidattan, N.R. Gopalakrishnan, P.K. Gopalakrishnan, T. Gopinath, Goscinni, L.A. Krishna Iyer, Prema Jayakumar, Robin Jeffrey, Radha Kamath, K. Krishnakumar, Ajithan Kurup, William Logan, N.S. Madhavan, Sree Padmanabha Dasa H.H. Marthanda Varma, K.P. Mayan, Sadanand Menon, A. Sreedhara Menon, M. Muralidharan, S.G.Nair, E.M.S. Namboodiripad, N.M. Namboodiri, K.C. Narayanan, M.G.S. Narayanan, Prem Nazir, T.K. Prakash, R. Prasannan, M.R. Rajan, T.K. Ramachandran, T.V.R. Shenoy, Sanjay Subrahmanyam, P.K. Michael Tharakan, Bonny Thomas, V.C. Thomas, Uderzo, C.R.R. Varma, Dr. Venu, Venu G, G. Vijayaraghavan, Shyama Warner, R.S. Whiteway, The Department of Tourism, Government of Kerala and friends in Th Indian Express Group.

WHAT YOU SEE

Asterix

Someone up there must surely have mixed feelings about this place. He gave Kerala a great geography and carpet-bombed it with history. From times difficult to date, the region has seen a steady stream of men engaged in every conceivable pursuit from business to pleasure. Explorers, invaders, proselytisers, traders, travellers, town planners, tourists and sundry seekers of well-being and nirvana.

Now, I join this formidable array with my sketchbook. But then, I belong to that special breed of non-resident Keralites. Kerala educates (or so we would like our employers to believe) and exports manpower. And we expats keep coming back whenever we can.

For us, Kerala is not a destination; it is an addiction. Come to think of it, it has been so for many others as well. Even Vasco da Gama, the most prominent visitor to drop by couldn't leave these shores for good. The hardy sailor found his way to this footnote of a land on the south-western Indian coast looking for preservative spices and Christian soulmates. He managed neither with any grace.

The trading and the ruling classes here were far more advanced and the local Christians far less Christian than he had bargained for. Calicut was no fiefdom of a tin-pot ruler. Commercial conventions and administrative protocols were very much in place. Not all locals were Christians as Gama had imagined and those who were looked like a freewheeling heterodoxy to Portuguese eyes.

To top it all this argonaut didn't time his historic touchdown well. He ought to have known better than to drop anchor as the southwest monsoon was just breaking over the Malabar Coast. More at home on a sail ship in the worst sea storm, the sailor wasn't quite the man for the rain-washed, slushy coastland. Dressed to the hilt in European regalia, his journey through pouring rain back to his lodgings after presenting his none-too-convincing credentials before Calicut's ruler, must have been quite a sight. Having refused a horse without a saddle that was offered to him, he was carried on the back by his men a good part of the way.

All this could have been pretty unsettling. Particularly for Gama, an impatient young achiever with a temper to boot. The Captain-Major was prone to become apasionado (livid) and perhaps swore as often and as colourfully as Captain Haddock does in the Tintin comics. Ultimately, Gama was to meet the destiny of his ilk – the larger-than-life figures of history. He became a comic character in the 1990s in a book, *Vasco da Gama e a India,* written and illustrated by two Portuguese artist-writers, Fernando Santos and Carlos Santos. Unlike the politically correct Haddock, the Portuguese seaman didn't stop at oceanographic swearwords.

Calvetti Bridge: Once the border between British Malabar and the princely state of Kochi; Fishermen mending net at Fort Kochi; Fishing at the Kochi waterfront.

Kannamali Church. Locals say the Portuguese built it and wonder whether the rundown structure will survive many more monsoons.

He unleashed sheer terror in these parts. Not the best of ways in the strangest of places to advance your business and religious interests.

To cut a long story short, Gama couldn't have gone back singularly jubilant over his discovery of Pepperland. But he came back older and none-the-wiser. Only, this time there was more method in his madness, thanks to the commercial pull of Malabar.

Finally, he came here a third time as Viceroy – to die soon after on Christmas Eve, 1524. And found little eternity thereafter. He lay buried in Kochi's Sao Francisco Church for a mere 14 years. His son, Dom Pedro da Silva Gama, exhumed his remains and took them to Portugal, where his bones haven't rested in peace in one place for long. They were shifted from one Portuguese monastery to another, first in 1880 and again in 1898. To make matters worse, doubts were cast on the identity of the bones that were transferred.

This is not to imply that an encounter with these shores can traumatise even posthumously. In the five centuries that have elapsed since the likes of Gama and Columbus set out on their grand voyages, the world has converged and Kerala has learnt to tease more subtly. But tease it will.

Even if you are a business traveller or a weekend visitor, you are unlikely to return with neat pic-

ture-postcard images. Why a weekend? Just a 10-minute walk from the Bishop's House to Fort Kochi's beach can affect you as few places can.

The town square in front of the Bishop's House is as humdrum as any. Nothing around looks particularly striking either. Some school kids are scurrying about. A couple of workers from the Municipal Office are out on their daily chore, wheelbarrow and all, to dispose of garbage. And a fishmonger arrives with his push-cart. Having nothing better to do, you follow him.

Into Lily Street. And you lose your moorings. No grand gothic structures here to dwarf you into touristy excitement. No weird men and women to make you reach for your camera. You are in an anywhere-on-earth lane, with rows of modest houses on either side. The kind you pass by without a thought. Nothing spectacular, nothing intimidating. Only, there is an anachronistic air about the place. And it seeps into you. You cross the road into the 17th century and shift your gaze into the 15th.

You have entered virtual space. The tropicalised European architecture along with the hybrid ethnicity of the people has woven a web around you. Click on a Dutch window and you reach 17th-century Amsterdam. Double click where Rose Lane appears with a brick-red cottage and you'll find yourself among the Jewish Diaspora setting up shop in Kochi in the 16th century.

Left (top to bottom):
Commuters in a boat that
does its routine run
between the tiny islands
off Kochi; Jose, Kochi's
"house painter", posing
for a portrait; This
young man is waiting
with his ice crusher
for the fishing boats to
arrive at Kochi harbour.

Fort Kochi beach. You can't shoot
Kochi without getting shot.

Ahead, you go round the Sao Francisco Church, where Gama was first buried, and cross more lanes hyper-linked to history and finally stop at the Chinese nets on the waterfront. A large fishing net tied to curved wooden arms counterbalanced by huge stones suspended to the other ends is alternately dipped into water and raised on shore by half a dozen men. Like a lazy kingfisher that stays rooted to a spot and dips its beak into water every now and then, this antique showpiece catches fish when the fish oblige. But there is a great deal of secondary activity around it. Hectic betting goes on before every haul on the size of the catch. And no camera-wielding tourist can resist the sky and the sea through the diaphanous net that balloons in the breeze.

At the end of your 10-minute walk through European, Jewish and Chinese space-time, you log out and look around. You are in for a bit of a comedown. A cameraman is shooting a documentary film on fisheries. Anticlimax never comes singly. Soon you realise that there is yet another with a camcorder videographing the filmmaker. And right behind him this cartoonist sits and records the multiple voyeurism, adding his doodling bit to it for good measure.

The 10-minute walk (pages 10-23): From the courtyard in front of Fort Kochi's Bishop House.

Turn to Lily Street.

Lily Street.

Lily Street ends.

Sao Francisco Church where
Gama was first buried.

Towards the back alleys of the church.

Behind the church.

On to Rose Lane.

Rose Lane.

The house of the late S. Kodar,
a prominent Jew of Kochi.

Chinese nets.

Fort Kochi beach.

Kochi can't keep its landscape to itself. Given its historic global links, anyone from any part of the world can claim a right over it. The Portuguese, the Dutch, the Jews, the French, the English... No wonder there is so much of overseas presence here. Foreign tourists arrive round the year even during the monsoons. Serially colonised by every European nation that rounded the Cape of Good Hope, Kochi doesn't hold it against them.

The tourist operator will tell you the town has gained more than it has lost. *He* has at any rate. And a lapse here or a misdemeanour there can surely be forgiven in *God's own country*. This is the tireless cliché in the tourist lexicon for Kerala. God, in fact, seems to be all over the place. Such omnipresence is singular, even by divine standards.

Did Keralites have more reasons to turn to Him than did people elsewhere? Almost every religion has its places of worship here. There are temples between churches and churches between mosques, not to speak of a Jewish synagogue almost nudging a Hindu temple in Mattancherry. Palayam in Thiruvananthapuram has a mosque and a temple sharing a wall and across the road from them is a church.

Jesus, Allah and the numerous gods of the pre-Hindu and the Hindu pantheon cuddle into this narrow land-strip much as the laity itself making tolerant coexistence the easier option.

Below:
View from Dutch Palace, Mattancherry. A Hindu temple and behind it a Jewish synagogue.

Opposite:
The Jewish synagogue, Mattancherry.

Inside Mattancherry Synagogue a foreign
tourist practices *pranayama*, a yogic exercise.

A church, a mosque and a temple cuddle into Palayam in the middle of Thiruvananthapuram.

If you have some sense of history, Kochi should leave you in a thanksgiving mood and you would head straight for Kodungallur. Kochi's glory as a port city began after 1341. When the Periyar River overflowed and silted the Kodungallur Port and created a natural harbour at Kochi.

If the stretch between Kochi and Kodungallur doesn't save your soul, nothing will. There is the riverside temple of Rama in Triprayar and a couple of magnificent ones of Shiva and Shakti in Kodungallur. The country's first mosque is here too. You'll see as you go along that the density of divinity gets a bit much.

The Cheraman mosque built in Muziris in AD 629 doesn't give away much history at first glance. Kerala's obsession with kitsch renovation has taken its toll. The façade with the mandatory minarets and arcades looks just about 20 years old. Pardonable because you soon realise that nothing about this region has remained quite the same – least of all its name. Once a thriving sea port, Muziris as it was known to King Solomon of Israel way back in 1000 BC, had a remarkably long stint at global commerce until the Periyar River misbehaved some six centuries back and wiped it off the trade map. Out of business, out of mind.

Meanwhile, the place had to put up with quite a bit of name-calling. There is a price to be paid for being historic. Muziris has been known to various people at various points in history as "Murachipattanam", "Muchiri", "Muyirikode", "Makotai", "Mahodayapuram" and "Mahodaya-pattanam". It finally changed to the present "Kodungallur" but not before going through yet another christening, "Cranganore".

Through all this and much more, the mosque couldn't have stood in timeless isolation. After the painted-up façade in concrete, the tiled structure behind looks almost ancient but can't be all that old. The Basel Mission mass-produced roofing tiles on the Indian west coast only in the 19th century. Banish such nit-picking. Once you are admitted into the prayer hall, everything from the carved doors to the priest's pulpit looks suitably ornamental and oldish. The mosque's most amiable authorities put it all down to the indigenous carpentry of the 7th century.

Having been anointed in legend, might as well soak in it. From the first mosque, the country's oldest church is just an hour and a prayer away. Kerala's narrow, winding, God-be-with-you roads take a bit of getting used to. At Palayur stands the oldest surviving Christian shrine on Indian soil. One of the seven churches, some believe was founded by Saint Thomas. The story goes that the Holy Apostle of Jesus landed in Muziris in AD 52 and impressed the local Brahmins (Namboodiris) with a miracle or two whereupon they promptly switched to Christianity. You can sample one such supernatural

Ornamental brass lamp inside the Triprayar Temple.

Inside Cheraman Mosque – the prayer hall
of the country's first mosque in Kodungallur.

The renovated façade hides the antiquity of Cheraman Mosque.

feat on the inside wall – a painting commissioned evidently in less hoary times. You see the saint waist deep in a village pond throwing a fistful of water up into the air where it stays suspended. Looking on is a group of Namboodiris, spellbound by this defiance of gravity. Only, one of them is wearing a shirt. In AD 52!

Most historians believe that Namboodiris came to Kerala centuries later and doubt if Doubting Thomas came here at all. And it is open to question whether at the advent of the Christian Era people in these parts had the kind of watertight religious identity that would motivate them to convert, miracle or no miracle. In fact, for the next several centuries they must have bowed before every shrine that came their way – from the pagan to the Buddhist and the Hindu. If it is conversion they went through, it is the kind the globetrotter undertakes today when he converts currency.

The Christians who eventually got here must have carried on in ways best known to them. The fact is that the region already had a home-bred Christian tradition when Vasco da Gama arrived, armed with a papal bull and a mariner's compass.

Those who feel far too strongly about such matters continue to spin yarns. Faster than the spider that promptly got into action as I stood and sketched the Palayur Church. In a mere half hour, it had appropriated me into the historic

Saint Thomas Forane Church in Palayur,
India's oldest Christian shrine.

Cheria Palli in Kottayam. This is one of the many Kerala churches that attracts non-Christians.

setting. A proper web had been woven between my drawing book and the foliage around.

Like any place that decks up to entertain visitors, Kerala likes to look good and old. Sometimes, older than the calendar would permit, often resulting in delightful anachronisms. Adoor Gopalakrishnan, the celebrated filmmaker, lives in the suburb of the state's capital in a timber and tile house he put together quite functionally from dismantled old buildings. He is far too serious a person to play pranks. But if he were to, the house can easily be passed off as a suitably old monument to which a touristy fairy-tale can be appended.

A similar new old structure has been built into the plantation landscape of Mundakayam, near Kottayam. A recent construction, the picturesque church in granite looks straight out of the 19th century. The local vandals have done their bit to enhance this architectural illusion. They have made off with the glass domes and electric bulbs from the lampposts, creating the look of neglect that goes so well with heritage.

While in these cases the retro look works, mostly it is neither aesthetic nor functional. Especially in combination with modern building materials. Keralites can't seem to leave concrete, steel and glass alone. They have to add cosmetic tiles, carved doors and decorative windows to needless pillars, columns and sloping roofs to produce unliveable space. In this

sunny land, it is darkness at noon in most workplaces when power fails. As for looks, while wood and tile get seasoned by the generous biannual showers and assume uncertain vintage, concrete doesn't age. Without proper upkeep, it only cracks and crumbles.

The mother of all architectural aberrations is there right in the middle of the state's capital. A city on seven hillocks, Thiruvananthapuram has a lovely undulating landscape dotted by some nice old buildings. It takes the government to make a difference. The new premises of the legislature are a straight tribute to Murphy's Law: If anything can go wrong, it will. Every housing norm from comfort to cost has been given the go-by. The exterior is weighed down by a surfeit of neo-antique Kerala motifs and half a forest must have been stripped to do up the interior.

If such are the affairs of state, the affairs of the Lord are curiouser. Temples, mosques and churches are built, rebuilt, enclosed or extended in a free fusion of designs from the past and materials that hardly match. The Thirumandhamkunnu temple in Angadipuram, rich in history and legend and without a compound wall, is getting renovated. Into what is best left to God himself. One of the low-roofed, non-intimidating twin temples in Panachikadu is a shrine of Saraswati, the goddess of knowledge. It is the most patronised centre in these parts for the formal initiation of children into learning.

A mandatory Hindu ritual that has come to cut across religions. When your child looks up after the customary scrawl on the rice spread in front, the sight that greets her won't be exactly edifying – a mass of plaster-pealing common-place concrete.

As you drive out of Thrissur towards Kochi, you freeze at the sight of Noah's Ark at Arimpur. On closer inspection the roadside biblical vision turns out to be a church modelled as a ship – resting mercifully on firm ground.

Given such institutional role models, ordinary folks can be pardoned their personal indulgences. They invest their lifetime earnings and worse, their lifetime art, into the houses they build. Make a house, the Keralite must. It has been an enduring obsession of this society. People here started living in proper houses much before did others in the neighbouring regions. Terra firma isn't all that firm in this rain-soaked land. It is mostly laterite. All you need is a hand tool or two to dig in and carve out building blocks. And dried palm leaves available in plenty make fine enough roofing material.

The high and mighty once showed off with tiled roofs made of baked clay. To begin with, only temples and palaces were allowed tiled roofing. By the 19th century, the Basel Mission set up tile factories and its market grew in a society that was reforming and beginning to distribute income. Eager commoners got access to tiles and made the most of it. To this day a good part of the remittances from the state's global Diaspora go into building and rebuilding.

Meanwhile Laurie Baker, an architect sensitive to local resources and possibilities, came up with the concept of low-cost housing – at once functional and stylish. Sure enough, Baker fakes rushed in to make a fast buck out of the emerging fad of low cost at any cost. The inmates of the split-level structural incongruities that ensued will tell you tales of leaking roofs, broken bones and a cleaned-out bank balance.

There are far too many Keralites in Kerala – some 750 crowd into a square kilometre. With increasing pressure on land, towns and cities are beginning to get inevitably vertical. Situated suitably, high rise can be high value for the realtor and the hotelier who sells you an eyeful – of more sky and more water than you will see if you were on a sailing ship. Such locations by the waterfront aren't hard to find. There are 44 rivers criss-crossing the state and several lakes, not to mention the 576-kilometre-long coastline. With so much of water around, Kerala has enough reason to worry and hope. Futurists, a famously undependable lot, foresee the next world war over water rights. In which case the place has had it. If, on the other hand, it is just a trade war the state will roll in hydro-dollars. With which every family will do one up on the neighbour's palace.

Renowned filmmaker Adoor Gopalakrishnan's house in Thiruvananthapuram.

Thirumandhamkunnu Temple,
Angadipuram, under renovation.

Saint Thomas Orthodox Church, Mundakayam.
The good old look reinvented.

The mother of all eyesores. The new legislative assembly building in the state's capital.

Noah's Ark? Saint Teresa's Church in
Arimpur on the Thrissur-Kochi highway.

The first house Laurie Baker
built in Kerala, Wagamon.

Commonwealth Tile factory, Palakkad.
One of the manufacturing enterprises
the Basel Mission brought to the
Indian west coast in the 19th century.

The samovar wasn't the only thing that was Russian about the Kerala teashop. Lenin, Stalin, Khruschev and Gorbachev have been assessed and reassessed here.

Kerala's romance with real estate has impacted, of all things, the media – both electronic and print. Television came when joint families had more or less split into nuclear units, which were discovering home, sweet home. Mom, dad and the kids were for the first time enjoying private space. Around the TV set came up a new comfort zone – the living room. A paralytic stroke couldn't have made the Keralite more homebound. Till the other day, he would build his house and promptly step out for a chat. More often than not, to the neighbourhood teashop.

A social anthropologist, Adrian C. Mayer, who researched Malabar in the 1950s says that the teashop played a significant role in subverting interdining caste taboos. More recently, through the 1960s, 1970s and 1980s students sipped endless cups of tea and chatted their way into Marx, Mao and Marquez. Social and political movements that needed to mass-mobilise found this congregational urge particularly useful.

The urge became more pronounced by sundown. Most men progressed from teashops to outlets that dispensed headier stuff. Women clustered in temples and churches. The more insular Muslim ladies too found an excuse to step out. They visited relatives, ailing or hypochondriac, in the variety of nursing homes every Kerala town has. There was no Kerala evening without a human figure trying to shape it. Hitting the football, lifting the volleyball,

rowing the little canoe, diving into the village pond or merely leaning against a lamppost, gesticulating most animatedly and talking, talking, talking.

It just took the TV to reverse all this. Now there is a near-total withdrawal from public spaces. TV couldn't have chosen a better time to come in. The broadly progressive politics that for long drove culture and entertainment has lost its pull. The Left radical has reached a cynical dead-end and the social democrat has run out of doles to distribute. Neither has the vocabulary to address an aspiring society. An uncertain brand of politics is waiting to be played out in the living rooms.

It is only a matter of time before cable TV reaches every Kerala home. It already has in pockets like Kumbanad, a suburb in siesta. Almost everyone here has either earned enough from stints abroad or has expat children who send large sums of money. From time to time during a commercial break, the senior citizens make their sole social contact. With the bank manager who has dropped in to get their fixed deposit renewed. They live their lives out in the living room, around talk shows, films and weepy soap the four TV channels in Malayalam compete to provide.

The print medium has benefited equally well from the housing boom. Nearly a 100,000 houses come up in Kerala annually and it has been so for 10 years. Which means a 100,000 more buy newspapers every year. This first fully literate Indian state goes to bed with TV and wakes up with the printed word. Newspapers seem to be produced much the same way as houses get built. The mindset is the same: fuse the new with what you imagine is the old. The result is a product mix of excellent production values and a retro-language that communicates by default. And the Malayali laps up this soap opera in print.

It is another matter that the Malayalam daily isn't the first choice of Generation Next, the first of its kind here being reared on TV, the Internet and English as preferred language. It will take a while for this trend to register.

Kottayam is the Mecca of print. Instead, should we say Vatican to underline the visible Christian presence? But then not all of the local Christians owe their allegiance to the Pope. Kerala's Christian community is a complex matrix of numerous denominations that will take several gigabytes to map out. The simpler option would be to meet Joseph Pulikunnel who heads Hosanna Publications. On matters Christian he is as irreverent as he is erudite. His mission in life seems to be to get under the skin of the bluffing and blustering priestly class.

Back to the print town. *Malayala Manorama* that outsells all non-English and most English language newspapers in the country, has its headquarters here. Yet another landmark is DC Books, Kerala's best-regarded publishing brand. Incidentally, they published this book. The organisation seems to have a risk-taking culture. The founder, the late D.C. Kizhakkemuri, saw publishing in Malayalam for what it is – the art of the impossible. He functioned in a literary minefield and kept peace with touchy writers, hypersensitive readers, hypertensive critics and a fair amount of genius. He had had an earlier stint at managing fragile egos as part of a core group that organised and ran a writers' cooperative (the SPCS). It published its members at a record 30 per cent royalty.

The sheer tonnage of print produce – newspapers, magazines and books – that roll out of this little town makes you wonder whether printing is the most productive activity in this industrially recalcitrant state. It all started with a hand-operated letter-press not much bigger than a confessional. Reverend Benjamin Bailey came here from London to work for the Christian Mission Society. He managed to accomplish a lot more than committees and consortia would today. He mastered the local language well enough to author books. He got local artisans to cast and mould Malayalam fonts that he himself designed and in 1821 set up the first press in Malayalam.

Since then all that the town has been doing is printing, publishing and grabbing headlines. Notching up one statistical glory after another.

First printing press in Malayalam installed by Reverend Benjamin Bailey in Kottayam in 1821.

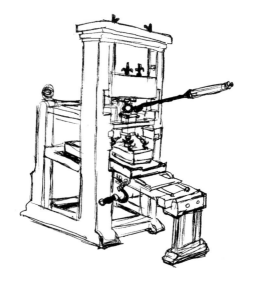

View of Kottayam Town
from DC Books.

Kerala's first college is here. The CMS College seems to have inspired the unlikeliest. Enough to make one of the least privileged students attend classes religiously. In Kerala circa 1940, he had everything against him from caste to cash. K.R. Narayanan went on to become a career diplomat and is now the country's president, the first Keralite to head the republic. The first Malayalam travelogue was printed in Kottayam. The first Malayalam dictionary, the first Malayalam-English dictionary, the first Malayalam Bible, the first Indian town to reach total literacy... Before "firsts" start coming out of your ears, duck the next statistic and flee.

To Kaduthuruthi, 20 kilometres from Kottayam. Where Kerala's martial art, *kalari*, teaches you to duck and defend rather than offend. In the sparse practising chamber of C.V.N. Kalari, E.P. Vasudeva Gurukkal sits on a stool and watches his students do feats, amazing to us and routine to him. He would make an excellent artist's model. But for the sharp gaze that darts across the gym to size up performance levels, the master is still as a statue. A perfect foil to the fast-forwarded choreography that is bursting all around him. To sketch these rhythmic, electrifying movements with some amount of accuracy, you need a persistence of vision enhanced many times over.

When Gurukkal demonstrates the use of *marma vadi*, the sheer power of suggestion is enough to have you in cold sweat. This seven-inch-long hand-held rod in rosewood almost disappears into the fist. Looks as innocuous as a yanked-out door handle. The knob that juts out between the forefinger and the middle finger is what does the job. A sharp jab and the opponent is history. This palmtop killer is best left to a master.

It needs years of practice and tons of attitude to attain the mastery and poise that Gurukkal has. He must be among the few hype-averse exponents left in *kalari*, which like the indigenous medical system, ayurveda, lends itself readily to exotic packaging. Evolved in times simpler, long before firearms erased personal valour from the art of battling, this form of combat worked often as a duel between mercenary warriors hired by feuding chieftains. *Kalari* heroes fought their own battles too for women and family honour.

Whether *kalari* won any war for Kerala or not, it did give Malayalam a repertoire of ballads – *vadakkan pattu*. Also it does seem to slow down ageing. At 73, Gurukkal looks a good twenty years younger and drives a jeep around with the reflexes of a 20-year-old.

Not all can take the long years of *kalari*'s rigour. An easier way to handle ageing is ayurveda. You just slip into a wooden cot, updated lately to fibreglass, and let the masseurs do the rest. You soak in oils treated with medicinal plants and come out smelling of a herbarium. This is

Right:
Vasudeva Gurukkal, the *kalari* master of
Kaduthuruthi, demonstrating the use of
marma vadi, the palmtop killer.

Left:
Students practising *kalari*, Kerala's martial art.

one of the standard ayurvedic cures – *sukha chikitsa*, comfort therapy, which is meant to rejuvenate you.

This homegrown healthcare system can reverse or arrest certain conditions modern medicine can't do much about like rheumatoid arthritis and stroke-induced debilities. And it does have palliative possibilities for terminal situations. A factor acknowledged by the team of allopathic doctors that run a centre in Kozhikode for pain and palliative care, the country's first.

All this is fine but no dramatic results here. You need patience and perhaps the right lifestyle. Ayurveda works best in its natural habitat. A couple of weeks in the nursing homes in Kottakkal or just across the state's border in Coimbatore or an hour with the Mooss in Thaikattusserry is enough to lull you into a pace the human body was perhaps designed for. If you have to speed and crawl through urban chaos for your daily massage, you will probably end up shedding more money than weight.

In a state forever in transition, ayurveda too has moved on. It has already progressed from back-yard home remedies to factory-made formulations. From inherited wisdom and familial control to broader organisational structures that network and manage. Now it is looking West. Where thanks to Chinese medicine, a market has opened up for herbal formulations. For anyone anywhere eager to look younger and feel better,

anything remotely herbal has come to be a religion – clean, no side-effects, even magical. Such singular faith doesn't go untapped.

Ayurveda is getting into the fast track. At a pace, the sceptic says, that isn't quite ayurvedic. Wonder cures are being freely advertised for modern-day maladies from hypertension to high cholesterol and HIV to hepatitis. Marketing guys are mouthing more R&D jargon than physicians. New pharma units are coming up by the dozen. But there is a twist in this hi-tech tale. Computerised, humidity-controlled, temperature-regulated, particle-free, factory floors haven't yet got rid of cauldrons filled with medicinal decoctions. The druid has still to stir up the magic potion. The past invariably catches up. Not just in ayurveda.

Inside the Malayali there seems to be a micro-Asterix. A subtle, subversive variation of the comic hero. Quite unlike the little Gaulish village conceived of by Goscinni and Uderzo, Kerala resists nothing consciously. If anything, it is only too eager to yield. If there were Romans surrounding it from all sides, it would have readily given in. The Romans would have rushed in and regretted it in ways far too complex for a comic book to delineate. Why, historians and anthropologists, into pursuits one trusts are far more serious than a comic book, are baffled by the micro-Asterix effect – a residual resistance to change. Ironically, brought about by an overdose of change.

Thaikattusserry Narayan Mooss, one of the last links with a familial tradition of ayurvedic medicine.

Arya Vaidya Sala in Kottakkal,
Kerala's capital of ayurveda.

The shop floor of a recently commissioned
ayurvedic pharma unit – modern in every
respect but the cauldrons of decoctions
are still around.

Cybele, a modern ayurvedic pharma
unit, with every state-of-the-art
trapping including landscaping.

Nearly every ethnic, social, religious, political, commercial and consumerist stream from anywhere in the world has some time or the other come into contact with this coastal land. Prompting people to constantly adapt, adopt and transform. And they did, at times more radically than most of Asia and parts of Europe. But then, how much of history can you take? The Malayali never got a break to assimilate anything thoroughly. He has had to stop short of breasting the tape and turn away to run another race. In the bargain he could neither accept nor reject anything fully.

It wasn't a wholly Buddhist Kerala that greeted Hinduism. It was a somewhat-Buddhist, somewhat-Hindu, somewhat-Muslim and Christian-of-sorts Kerala that confounded Vasco da Gama. It will take a longer string of prefixes to describe the Kerala that took to Marxism. Kerala history picks up prefixes and relics as it goes along. If you are looking for a neat civilisational pattern, look someplace else. The little Asterix acts up to upset the best-laid bookish plans.

Unlike the Gaulish Asterix, the Malayali Asterix extends endless courtship. But no marriage. This is how he approached everything that came his way from clothes to culture. Even as recently as 20 years ago, half of Kerala wore unstitched cloth. Most men wrapped a white or off-white *mundu* around the waist and many women wore a two-part variant of it. Some men went about topless and so did the odd

woman. Shirts, trousers, blouses and the pan-Indian sari were all there but were not uniformly accepted. The Sunday painter's limited colour palette was good enough to capture Kerala. If he wasn't too fussy and arty, he could do with marine blue, sky blue, brown tints, plenty of green and even more of red for the flags that fluttered from every factory gate.

Since then red has faded but overall the scene has become more colourful. White and off-white have given way to a variety of printed and dyed shades. Women seem to have waged a sartorial war against the male gaze. *Salwar-kameez* has replaced the sari as a more functional workaday wear. If cleverly tailored this two-part apparel conceals even better than the sari. More and more Muslim women are disappearing more and more into the cassock-like purdah, colourful ones though. Back home, almost every woman slips into what is called the nightie. This short-sleeved, loose hanging cloak that comes down to the ankles isn't strictly homebound. It floats freely into the near and the not-so-near neighbourhood.

The men aren't lucky enough to find a cover-all fashion wear. The older they get, the trendier they dress. Many in that desperate state of middle age try out the latest branded shirt, T-shirt, jeans that cling and trousers that bag hoping to somehow distract your gaze from their waistline. The place is a good hunting ground for the garment dealer.

This young woman in a "nightie" runs a teashop. Primarily a home-wear, the "nightie" floats freely into the neighbourhood and even into the workplace.

But all this doesn't mean the good old unstitched cloth has finally gone away. On the numerous occasions that mark the Malayali social life from baptisms to birthdays and weddings to festivals, it surfaces. Men wear the *mundu* but with a waist belt to hold it in place and the professional beautician helps the younger women with their *mundu* set or sari.

If every relic has a place in the Malayali's wardrobe, his mind can't be any different. See how he skirted the law of social development. In the middle of patriarchal succession came up matriliny, an essentially tribal practice that thrived here mostly among the Nair community for a good thousand years. Right into the modern times of private property, English education and foreign travel.

Again, look at the way Kerala handled religion after religion. Christianity came here in waves across centuries but neither Vasco da Gama in 1498 nor the Synod of Diamper (Udayamperur) in 1599 could bring the entrenched stream of Syrian Christians under the Pope. Led by Alexis De Menezes, the Archbishop of Goa, 813 delegates gathered at Udayamperur for that very purpose. They thought all irritants including that peculiar Hindu legacy called caste would instantly vanish under the common papal umbrella. Far from it. What ensued was bitterness and eventually a backlash. In 1653, Syrian Christians gathered in Mattancherry around a cross, tied to it a rope long enough for several

to clasp and took a vow once and for all to have nothing to do with the Vatican. This has come to be known as the *Coonan Kurisu Sathyam* – the Oath of Coonan Cross.

This vertical split didn't remain vertical for long. More splintering occurred horizontally and diagonally, spawning numerous Christian denominations. Some of them went so far as to seek court orders on their divine (and property) rights. Forcing Christian and non-Christian judges to learn Syriac and Latin more thoroughly than the clergy itself. Their Lordships had to arbitrate over matters intricate and liturgical. Apart from this limited dissemination of mothballed languages, Christian diversity gave Kerala a range of church architecture.

Kerala's Jain and Buddhist legacies can't be recounted with such detail or certainty. These religions flourished here in less-documented times – till about the 9th century. Pundits say that Jains who came here were keener to contemplate and meditate than to pressure-sell religion. But Jainism did find quite a few patrons among the ruling classes and the common folk. How, one wonders. The Keralite then ate, drank and served his gods more meaty and heady stuff than Jainism permitted. He must have added one more doctrine, suitably customised, to his expanding repertoire of divinity and continued to invoke deities of every persuasion.

This delightfully confused state of affairs has

Inside the Jain Temple, Palakkad.

All Saints Synod Church, Udayamperur, where in 1599 a vain attempt was made to bring all Kerala Christians under the Vatican.

left behind Hindu shrines, that must have been Jain to start with, temples and mosques with tell-tale signs of Jain architecture and quite a few Jain families. The Malayali Asterix added another set of relics to his collection.

Buddhists, more single-minded propagandists than Jains, created a better base for themselves in the region. Well earned because they made a developmental impact. Theirs, at any rate before the *tantric* phase, was a down-to-earth theology that targeted commoners. To their temples they attached primary schools and ayurvedic healthcare centres. Kerala has something to thank them for. The state was later to build up on these early starts to reach Euro-grade literacy and public health on income levels woefully Asian.

Buddhists are also credited with the introduction of the plough in southern India. Jains too had encouraged farming but were averse to Mother Earth being dug up. They couldn't have approved of even the digging stick of the local tribes, leave alone the plough. The plough must then have meant as much to Kerala society as the steam engine to 18th-century England. Besides the plough, Buddhism also left behind a deity, Ayyappan, now worshipped as the Hindu god Sastha, who attracts an ever-growing mass of pilgrims from all over the country and even outside.

Buddhism also brought in the monastic order –

During the annual festival at Sabarimala the deity, Ayyappan, becomes a mandatory display on the tens of thousands of vehicles that ferry the pilgrims.

Hydrose Koya Thangal carries on his Muslim family tradition of healing by prayer.

which some say was later adopted by the Christians. It certainly became a more immediate favourite with Adi Sankara, who went on to establish four monasteries to propagate the faith countrywide. He transfused so much of Buddhism into Hinduism that he has been called a crypto-Buddhist (*prachanna-Buddha*). This 9th-century proponent of monism (*advaita*) merged diverse religious rituals, practices and precepts across the country into a pan-Indian Hindu brand.

Sankara travelled widely to meet and debate with scholars and won over every opposing or dissenting school of thought. Whereupon he is believed to have ascended the seat of omniscience (*sarvajnapeetham*) with the words "master of all but astrology", implying that stars can't foretell personal fortunes with any precision. Perhaps the last tentative note in a Malayali scholar. Since then Kerala has never stopped debating – often to distraction – with much less scholarship and even less humility. Sankara himself has been a victim of this. Every evil from caste system to untouchability has been imputed to him. A matching payload of divinity has been bestowed on him too. No way you can sensibly approach the formidable body of work this man who lived for a mere 32 years is credited with.

Islam has come to be seen here with even more passion and a lot less sense. Trade winds brought this religion to these shores in the 7th or 8th century – live from Arabia even as the Prophet's direct disciples were preaching. Since the likes of Taliban have now given it a bad name, a good deal of pedantic energy is expended to oppose or defend every Islamic issue in terms of us and them. Only a 1300-year-old Keralite can rightfully see Islam as alien. Though Kerala can boast of a steadily improving life expectancy, it hasn't produced a Methuselah yet. In any case, what could be alien to the Malayali's cocktail ethnicity?

Mercifully, multiethnic genes aren't easily driven by adrenaline. You find ordinary folks more relaxed in these matters. In Kappad, off Kozhikode, where Vasco da Gama first landed in 1498, a local Muslim who mans a phone booth mocks the self-styled anti-imperialist who lands up every once in a while to vandalise the abandoned monument to this sailor. Across the road, the faithful who have gathered for their midday prayer at the mosque endorse him. The local Muslims can find enough reasons to get worked up against the Portuguese sea-man but they choose not to. "Why should we bother about who did what to whom centuries ago?" they ask, "if the place is developed into a tourist spot, at least the roads will improve."

Soon you realise that the past does mean a lot to Kozhikode – in a harmless sort of way. Everything about the place looks sepia-tinted. People seem to be wallowing in nostalgia. Ever ready to commemorate and celebrate any

The European dream voyage in search of an all-sea trade route to this spice coast ended here. Vasco da Gama landed in this beach in Kappad, off Kozhikode in 1498.

Right:
The abandoned monument to
Vasco da Gama in Kappad.

event that can be divined from the calendar. From the birth/death anniversaries of Kunjali Marakkar, the local hero who fought the Portuguese, to Kundan Lal Saigal, the singing star of early Hindi cinema.

When Gama arrived looking for pepper, Kozhikode was Malabar's best-known port of exchange. Virtually a free port, Portuguese records refer to it as "Calecute", which with more European exposure got standardised as "Calicut". By an early account, the local ruler was "Samudri Raja" (the king of the seas). The Portuguese called him Samorim and the Europeans who followed subjected the honorific to many twists and turns till it eventually became Zamorin. Before long, the bearer of the title was reduced to a pensioner-prince of the British Crown.

But in the 15th century, the Zamorins were in an expansionist mood. They needed all the money they could make out of overseas trade to expand over land. What is statecraft for, if it can't yield an enemy or two? The Zamorin had a bone to pick with the Kolathiris in the north and a major feud with Kochi in the south. Their trade-driven liberal policy was hospitality at its best. It proscribed nothing but cow slaughter. In the bargain, Calicut's marketplace must have ended up looking like an everyday costume ball. Bustling with merchants in Arab attire, brokers in Gujarati wear, Europeans out of a Renaissance painting, the royal constabulary wielding swords

Mochundi Mosque, Kozhikode. The indigenous *vasthu* architecture has been preserved but for the mandatory appendage – the loudspeaker.

The shipyard at Beypore which has a
centuries-old tradition of building sailing
vessels now gets an occasional order
from the adventure tourist.

and shields, entertainers with pipes and drums and semi-literate interpreters who added to the general mirth.

Centuries of commerce and culture have left behind more footprints in Calicut's mind than in its landscape. The neatly whitewashed head-quarters of the Commonwealth Industries at the city centre seems a clear instance of mind over matter. Should make a unique case study in management. Mainly into textiles and tiles, the company is saddled with a massive work-force that ties in with 19th-century productiv-ity norms. It can't downsize because the Basel Mission Trust, which owns the concern, has no such provision. It had the evangelical commit-ment to employ fresh converts from the local outcastes. A minor Christian miracle that the establishment still runs. Together with the stretch of dilapidated warehouses along the beach road proclaiming one-time mercantile glory, it should make an excellent setting for a period *boxwallah* film.

There is no trace of the Zamorin's palace. Thank god because this modest building (by one account a mere 2500 square feet) would have been an embarrassment today. Many petro-dollar-earning families live in more palatial houses and the state's Marxist party owns more extensive real estate in most towns.

Palaces apart, Calicut hasn't retained those un-mistakable signs of warring regimes, forts. In

A member of a workers' cooperative in Kalyassery rolling beedis (country cigars). The Marxist Party which runs several such units needs to reinvent itself as much as the tobacco trade.

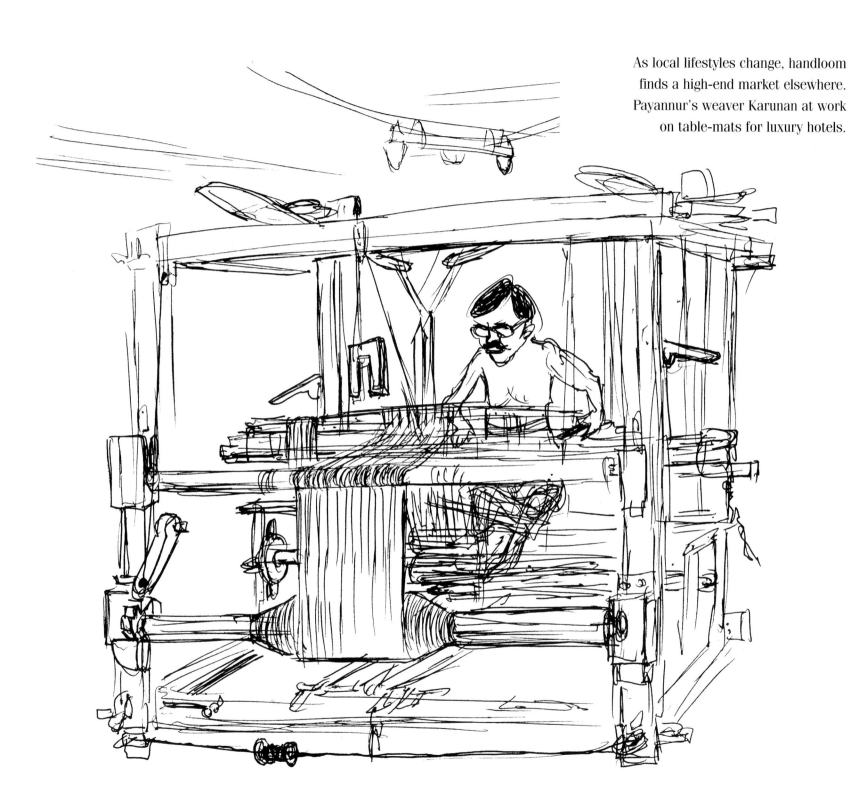

As local lifestyles change, handloom finds a high-end market elsewhere. Payannur's weaver Karunan at work on table-mats for luxury hotels.

the neighbouring Tellicherry, there is one built by the English and the triangular 16th-century fort the Portuguese built in Kannur is a favourite picnic spot. Makers of movies and young couples inspired by them head further north towards Bekal. Jutting out into the sea, with a fine beach at its foot, Bekal Fort was built in the 17th century by Sivappa Naickan to resist every assault except the one by the camera. With lines, levels and a horizon that constantly tease the eye, there are optical illusions here for the asking. And the cameraman freaks out on the kind of freewheeling visual incongruities that mark Indian cinema.

The equally scenic High Range attracted men who came in pursuit of more steady commerce than cinema. The Gama who "discovered" the Kanan Devan Hills in 1790 was Colonel Arthur Wellesley, the Duke of Wellington. He was on Operation Tipu Sultan. The Mysore Prince had given him the slip and on his way back to base camp the colonel halted here. In the few days he was here his little band of soldiers began work on a fort, which was perhaps an excuse to hang around in the cooler hills – a closer home weather for the Duke. But before it could be built he got orders to move on.

It took another 90 years for an officer of the Travancore state, John Daniel Munro, to sight the commercial possibility of the High Range. He bought 227 square miles of land from the Poonjar Raja. For part of the land Munro raised

The English Church (opposite) and its cemetery (below) in Tellicherry. You have to scale the wall and wade through wild grass to take a good look at this historic site.

An offshore coconut grove you can
walk across to in low tide, Dharmadam.

Bekal Fort – seems to have been built for the
song-and-dance sequences of Indian films.

Rs 5000 and committed himself to an annual payment of Rs 3000. The civil service in the 1870s must have been enviably looked after. No wonder in these parts it remained the first career option for a long time to come.

Munnar still retains a misty European air. It is quite a while since the Europeans hung their hats at the High Range Club and left. There are 51 hats on the bar wall. A planter puts in 30 years of unbroken service to merit this honour. The 52nd hat is unlikely to grace the teak-panelled wall, though. Today the Tea Township is run by the Tatas. They have to shuffle man-power across a diversified corporate. The bot-tomline matters more than the High Range. However, through periodic transfers, the Tatas have ended up promoting Tamil. Unsuspecting youngsters from far-flung Punjab and Kashmir, the occasional tough lady included, get posted to Munnar where they have to interact with the overwhelmingly Tamil-speaking labour in a Dravidian language older and more alien to the north Indian tongue than English.

Unlike their predecessors who left their hats on the club wall, these young managers don't carry home Munnar memories quaint enough to enter-tain their grandchildren. The odd numismatist among them won't add that rare coin to his col-lection. The Kanan Devan Hills Produce Com-pany once minted its own wage tokens to make sure the workers didn't bolt with the wages. The coins were valid only within the corporate empire, which had devised an even more origi-nal method of risk-free, pilfer-free, theft-free money transfer. The currency notes were cut in half and the halved lot was sent to the estates. Once the truncated notes completed their jour-ney safely across cumbersome cart tracks the other halves were despatched.

While such High Range exotica are a thing of the distant past, the ecology is still worth writ-ing home about. The highest Indian mountain peak south of the Himalayas is here in Anamudi. The High Range loyalist often voices a fond hypothesis that if the peak were higher and God kinder, Kerala could have had snow. And all that comes with it from skiing to a white Christmas. The tourists would have loved it and the expat Keralite on his mandatory homecoming could have snow-capped his already rain-soaked and lush green nostalgia.

Kerala is unique in that it is a favoured desti-nation of its own people. A good many men and women from here work outside the state and spend annual or biennial holidays back home. Often carting along sundry gadgetry from the world markets. They have been the unpaid salespersons for a range of global products and brands. The state's countryside got exposed to fancy wristwatches, blaring music systems and the yet-to-be tropicalised washing machines ahead of most cities and towns in the rest of the country. Thanks to this demonstration effect, the Malayali is quite impressionable to

Tea plucking in Munnar.

Munnar's tin-roofed Christ Church in granite, founded in 1910, now run by the Catholics of South India.

sales talk and Kerala is a test-marketing ground for any new product or service.

Between holidays, the expat sends home money and these remittances drive trade and consumerism rather than industry and employment. All the brick and mortar go into buildings that house the neo-nuclear family units, multiplying trading outfits, mushrooming healthcare and teaching shops and gods of every faith and sub-faith. Not much room left for boilers and assembly lines. Successive governments have missed out on the Old Economy and this has had its rewards!

When you opt for a shop window that is a lot cleaner than the factory chimney, you are left with a busy marketplace and not much industry to pollute. Industry or no industry, clean air is certainly not a bad thing. And there is at least one industry that loves it – tourism. As always, the good old Asterix factor – the subterranean resistance to change – won the day.

More recently, the state missed the non-polluting IT-bus too. This is despite the initiative to set up the country's first techno-park and an eminently upgradable skill base to draw upon. Never mind. Soon enough hindsight will reveal that the economy has escaped the inevitable boom-and-bust cycle of neo-capitalism. The little Asterix saved Kerala from the brick-and-mortar rat race and now from the click-and-portal mouse race. At the end of our drive through K-Towns – from Kochi, Kodungallur, Kozhikode, Kottayam, Kannur down to the Kannan Devan Hills – we find that he has had his way. Asterix has made sure that the state keeps falling between stools and somehow lands on all fours. Now, over to Cacofonix. ◆

The bar at the High Range Club.
Fifty-one planters who served in Munnar
for an unbroken 30 years hung
their hats on the bar wall and left.

The typical tea estate manager's
bungalow in Munnar.

Tata Tea Factory, Munnar – women workers
coming to work as day breaks and the mist lifts.

Sri Padmanabhaswami Temple,
Thiruvananthapuram.
The erstwhile Travancore State
was dedicated to the deity
of the temple.

Museum junction at the
centre of Thiruvananthapuram.

Kanakakunnu Palace, Thiruvananthapuram.

Once the summer palace of
Travancore royalty, film crews
looking for a period setting often
rent this bungalow in Kuttikkanam.

Connemara market, the crumbling landmark
in Palayam, Thiruvananthapuram.

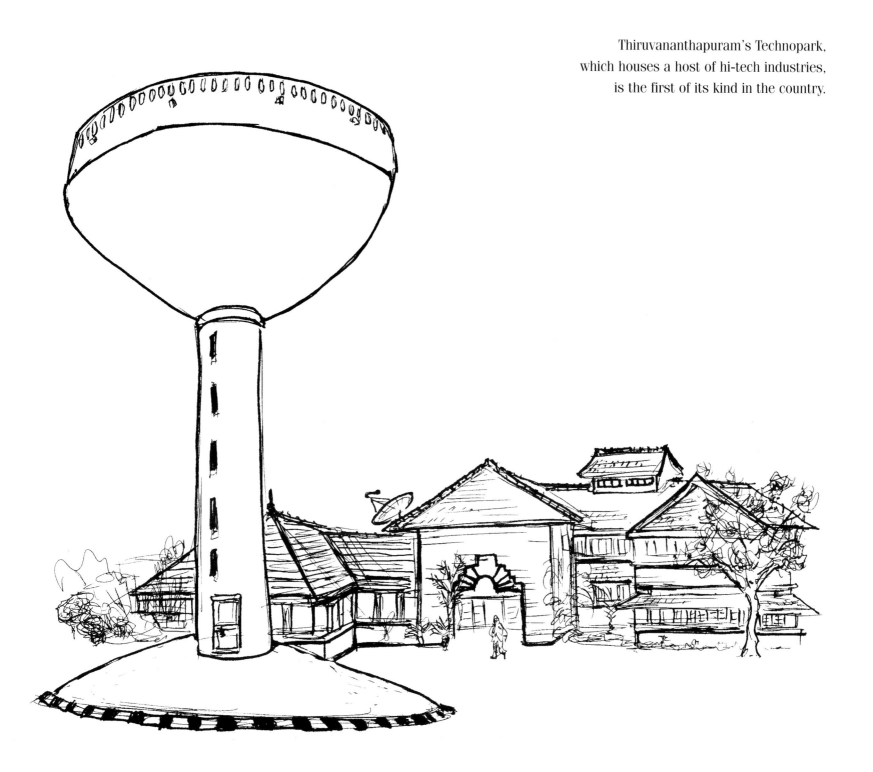

Thiruvananthapuram's Technopark,
which houses a host of hi-tech industries,
is the first of its kind in the country.

Fishermen relaxing over a card game
called "Earth" in Azheekkal, Kollam.

Chinnakada, Kollam. The kind of export earning this Cashew Town has had is hardly visible in this marketplace.

A Kottayam morning.
Joggers and church-goers.

This temple in Panachikadu for Saraswati, the goddess of knowledge, is a favourite place for the ritual initiation of children into learning.

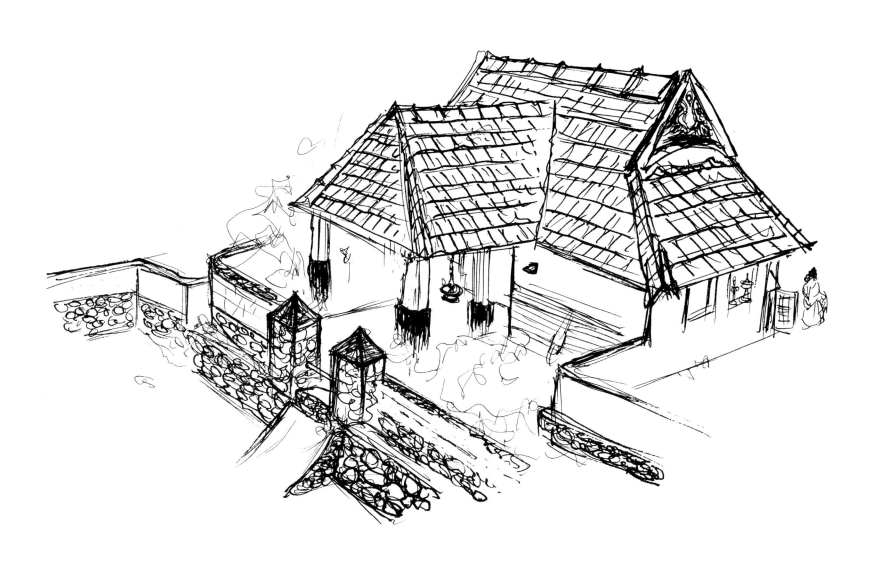

Abbot Francis Acharya, the Gandhian priest from
Belgium who founded the Kurisumala Ashram.

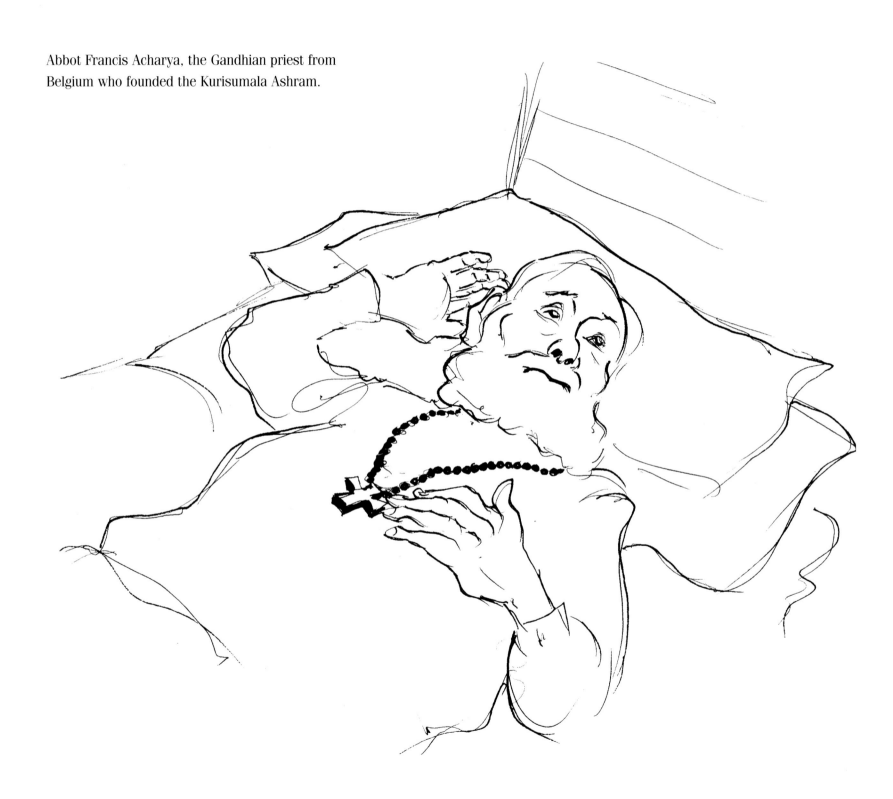

The historic Brunton Boatyard renovated
by the Casino Group into a heritage hotel
on the waterfront in Fort Kochi.

Aspinwall & Company, part of the
Old World Kochi's mercantile glory.

View of Mattancherry market from the
Customs Jetty, Willingdon Island.

Fishing harbour, Kochi.

An eyeful of Kochi harbour from
Taj Malabar Hotel, Willingdon Island.

Swarnath Mana, a wealthy Namboodiri
household with an austere, time-frozen lifestyle.

Tirumala Devaswam Temple in Cherlai, Kochi,
patronised by the Konkani community.

This small-time hawker's meagre margins come out of a trade map bigger than the European Union. Lal Mohammed from Gorakhpur, Uttar Pradesh spends four to five months in Kerala selling bamboo flutes made in Assam.

Kunnakulam. Rightly or wrongly dubbed the Duplicate Town, it has a reputation for counterfeiting any branded product.

Thrissur was a temple kingdom
(*ambalarajyam*) built around the
Vadakkunnathan Temple.

Koothambalam at Thrissur Vadakkunnathan Temple. Classical performing arts like *Kootiyattam*, the stylised Sanskrit drama, are performed in this temple-theatre.

The four centres established by Adi Sankara in Thrissur for vedic studies. Much later in the 20th century, the standoffish Namboodiri community was to reform majorly from here.

Inside the *koothambalam* in Kalamandalam, the premier centre for training in the traditional performing arts of Kerala.

Ammanur Madhava Chakyar,
the last of the masters of
Kootiyattam. This 2000-year-
old Sanskrit theatre has
survived in Kerala despite
its unhurried performing
pace. It takes an eternity
to bat an eyelid here.

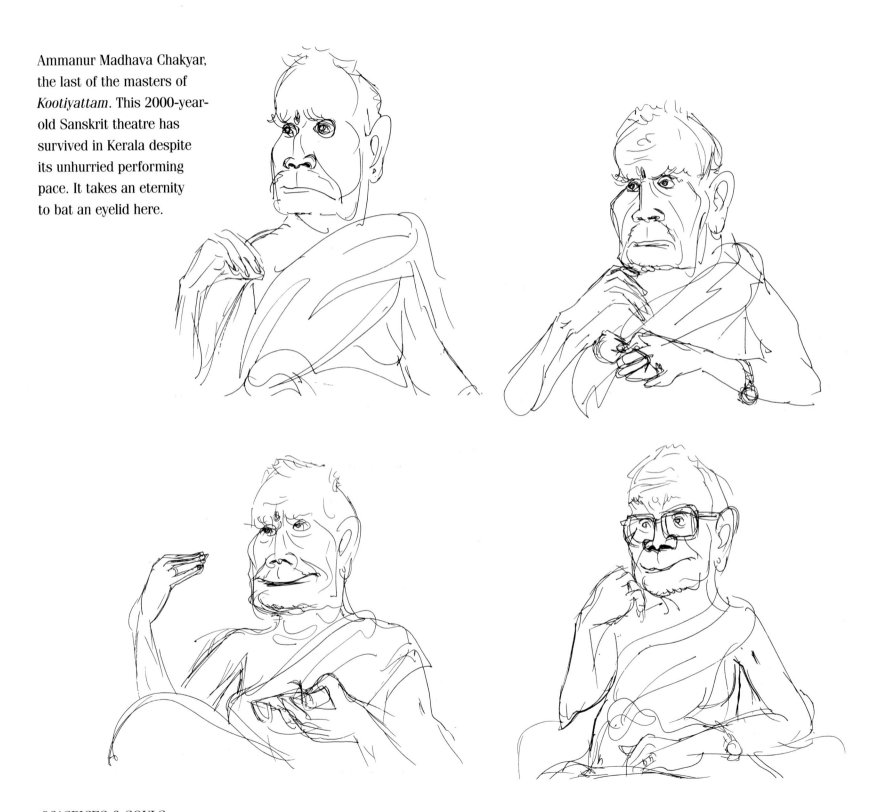

Ammanur's only diversion seems
to be these cows. He stops to
exchange eloquent glances with them.

Kathakali master Ramankutty Nair says a brief prayer and gets ready for the elaborate make-up characteristic of this theatre form.

On the make-up room mat,
the actor dozes off...

...To wake up as the character.

In her ancestral house, this elderly lady
waits for the night to darken and the
Thiruvathira festivities to begin.

Thiruvathira kali – a 1000-year-old tradition of
women staying up through the night, singing and
dancing to propitiate Shiva.

WHAT YOU HEAR

Cacofonix

Has Kerala had a recent war or famine? Once in every while a vehicle whizzes by carrying coffins, in twos and fours. And you often find huge black ones serially lined up on either side of the highway. On a closer look, the wooden contraption turns out too rectangular to be a coffin. It is what people here call the box mike – actually a box speaker. It underlines mortality of another kind – the death of the quiet moment. Silence is too much to ask for in a place with such a high density of population, every section of which has been empowered to speak up. In this democracy of decibels, the louder the better.

Cacofonix reigns. Nothing happens quietly here, not even daybreak. The Kerala morning is best enjoyed with earplugs on. You are never far from temples and mosques. And loudspeakers have become integral to their architecture. Hindu devotional songs rendered off-key by the overused audio tapes and discs fuse with the similarly dissonant Muslim morning prayer to produce a sonic boom which will make you long for the factory siren. The churches are kinder. They spare the non-enthusiast. Their megawatt speakers are directed only at the faithful who congregate for the morning mass.

As the day wears on, more pieces are added to the orchestra. The advertiser drives around in a jeep fitted with a noise box to announce the arrival of the umpteenth jewellery shop in Alappuzha, an industrial ghost town. If you can't produce and consume like a modern society, produce noise and consume gold. From his meandering three-wheeler, the political factotum wields the mike to warn the citizen on the next statewide *bandh*, the cessation of work and all commercial activity, a frequent expression of protest politics in these parts. Even the pavement vendor hawks through a battery-powered megaphone.

Try calling on elders and you will be most unwelcome. Amidst the steady din from the TV set, you won't get any eye contact. Kerala has a considerable greying, hair-dyeing and TV-viewing population. So remote-savvy that it switches from one Malayalam channel during the commercial break to catch glimpses of the soap or the films that are going on in the other three. You are left to cope with a multiple soundtrack that builds up in the living room.

Indoors and outdoors the Malayali can't seem to function without ambient noise. If this macro-noise isn't enough, there is micro-noise too. After TV, the gadget that Kerala has taken to with matching passion is the mobile phone. Not without reason. The typical Malayali home has an overseas member or two to keep up with and cellphone tariffs are cheaper. Also, this narrow land strip is geographically cut out to be wired up and smart. People are compulsively talking into mobile networks. Smoking

This advocate of scientific temper is holding forth through a deafening public address system to a polite and bored roadside audience.

Politics as noise. Every political party
seems determined to make itself heard
at such street-corner meetings.

has been banned here in public places. Is the cellphone a substitute for the cigarette? It keeps your hand and mouth engaged. If for some reason mobile phones disappear from the market, many would be walking around waving their free hand in the air and talking to themselves, in need of de-addiction.

That is an extreme possibility. But the fact is that the Malayali feels more comfortable talking to a remote listener through a machine interface. The microphone, the amplifier, the box speaker or the phone, mobile or landline. After some fifty years of airing more radical and inventive political ideas than have been heard in any other part of the country, the political voice has turned into noise. The leader shouts into the mike one-liners for the media to pick up and slogans for the hired crowds to repeat. Meanwhile more eager audiences seek spiritual high through the box speakers at congregations addressed by faith healers, wheelers and dealers.

Even small talk is difficult to sustain face to face, leave alone conversation. Perhaps the last time Kerala celebrated the art of conversation was in Kodungallur. The local royalty, a learned lot, ran a study centre here modelled on the traditional *gurukula* system – an unstructured way of learning through oral instruction and debate with the masters. By the 19th century end it became a powerhouse that energised Malayalam language and literature. The most

athletic of the scholastic feats undertaken at the centre was by Kunjukuttan Thampuran. He dictated to a retinue of scribes the instant Malayalam translation of the epic Mahabharata, over a 100,000 Sanskrit quatrains in all, in 874 days flat. Pundits aver that he retained and arguably bettered the poetry of the classic he sourced.

Today, the Kodungallur Palace is abandoned and silent. Its tradition of straight and lively Malayalam hasn't found a new voice. The media industry with a captive literate statewide market never bothered to build up on it. The last stylebook in the language is of World War II vintage, published in 1942, by Kutti Krishna Marar. Little wonder that today some of the finest young minds are migrating not just from Kerala but from Malayalam to English. Which Internet-savvy youngster would hold on to a language that has more speed-breaking adjectives and metaphors than roller-skating verbs?

If this has been the fate of the spoken word, Kerala's music has a more checkered history. Strangely, the coastland that was open to direct Western influences for over half a millennium didn't imbibe much European music. A bit of choir and carol singing and even less of classical Western music came in. Unlike Bengal, which thanks to the British Raj developed a parallel system of writing scores, Kerala has no written music. And the Christmas carol of the new millennium seems a spirited take-off on

Coat of arms of the Kodungallur royalty.

Kodungallur Kovilakam – once a great centre of
learning, now deserted and overgrown with wild grass.

peppy film tunes. This part of theology has at any rate been liberated from piety.

If the coastline itself was of little help, the Western Ghats could have been only a natural wall to music. Ironically some music came through these mountain passes – mainly the one in Palakkad. Tamil Brahmins brought Karnatak classical music and conserved it in their uniquely organised settlements called *agraharams*. Facing rows of wall-to-wall houses on either side of an open corridor that ends in a temple sustained a community lifestyle that was typically half closed and hence half open.

Unlike the Malayali Brahmins (the Namboodiris), their Tamil-speaking counterparts were less bound by the caste norms of unapproachability and unseeability. They mixed more freely with commoners because they had to work for a living. They had a slant for the kind of disciplines that got better with practice. From the hyper-structured Karnatak music to culinary skills. They ran eateries, which gave the Malayali with hardly anything sweet on his menu the sweet tooth. Also, they taught him Stenography to Shakespeare and Mathematics to Music.

Under this less standoffish knowledge aristocracy, Karnatak music eventually found favour with a society that was getting to be egalitarian. For the aspiring classes it was attainable elitism. The less fortunate got it between their

eyes from the popular Tamil drama, replete with high-pitched songs. With all this, Karnatak music never quite became a mainstream tradition in Kerala. Like all skills, it too catered to the state's primary economic activity – manpower export. The best of Palakkad's musical talents found patronage elsewhere. Palakkad Anantha Rama Bhagawathar, Mundazhi Rama Bhagawathar, Palakkad Mani Iyer, Chembai Vaidyanatha Bhagawathar, Palakkad K.V. Narayanaswami, Palakkad Raghu, Pudukkode Krishnamoorthi and Manjapra Devesa Ramanathan packed up and left carrying the names of their hometowns as baggage tags.

Similar tales will be recounted to you from the other islands of music in the state. Violinist Sundaram Iyer left Paravur and went all the way to Benares to accompany Omkar Nath Thakur. His violin-playing sons M.S. Anantharaman and M.S. Gopalakrishnan live in Chennai. Narayana Iyer from a musical family in Tripoonithura trained the violinist son in Karnatak and the violinist daughter in Hindustani classical music. Professor T.N. Krishnan and sister Dr N. Rajam visit their home state when invited to perform. Those who have stayed back to teach or work for the local radio stations like Neyyatinkara Vasudevan and Pala C.K. Ramachandran get no support that matches their competence.

Kerala doesn't seem to have a particularly musical ear. All hell will break loose if you make this statement within earshot of the Malayali

From these most ordinary street houses in Manjapra, Palakkad, emerged some of the biggest names of Karnatak classical music.

The sit-out of the late Chembai Vaidyanatha
Bhagawathar's house facing the village temple.

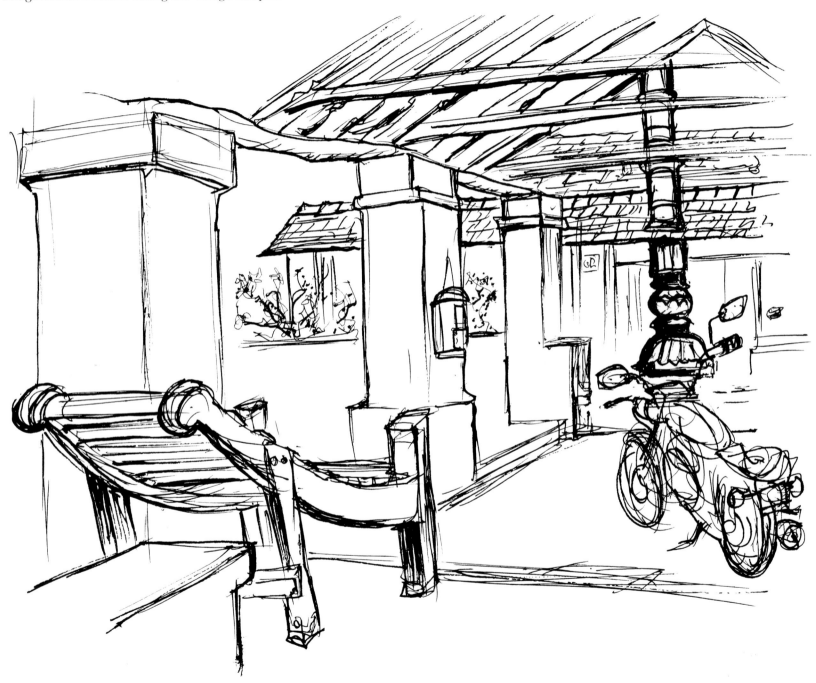

School-going girls practising Karnatak
music in Tharakkad, Palakkad.

At the 43rd annual painting contest organised
by the Universal Arts in Kozhikode's indoor
stadium, children relax and paint thanks to
the organisers who keep the anxious
parents and teachers out.

KPAC, a theatre troupe that came up with the state's left-wing politics.

culture enthusiast. Cut to the quick, he will rebut your view citing the indigenous tradition of *sopana* singing, the dance music of Kathakali and Mohiniattam and the percussion ensembles with their intricate rhythmic scales. He will go on and on about the *edakka*, a drum whose vibrating volume is varied to suggest melody. He will get worked up over KPAC, a left-wing theatre group which gave away some gifted musicians to cinema and left behind a repertoire of nostalgically recalled songs. All this is fine but where are the listeners?

There are keener event managers than performers and there are more performers than listeners here. In spite of its early exposure to amplifying and loudspeaking equipment, the state hasn't even a couple of acoustically passable chambers for listening. But there is no dearth of culture fests, where crooning is part of the package. The most hysterical of these events are the annual youth festivals for school- and college-going kids. Where if your child fails to win a prize, suicide is considered an option. The stakes are hyped up to the extent of petitioning the courts on the fairness of assessment by the prize-awarding jury. Such parental anxiety drains any art, music or childhood left in the child.

However, against all odds, music does survive in certain pockets – like underground movements. There is one right in the middle of the state's capital. Adjacent to the Sri Padmanabhaswami

Temple, a little chamber that is part of a palace belonging to Travancore's erstwhile ruling family becomes a venue for a unique musical experience. For a mere nine evenings in a year – during the Navaratri festival – handpicked Karnatak musicians sing or play on the veena compositions of Maharajah Swati Tirunal, the legendary artistic prince who ruled Travancore in the 19th century.

There is a loudspeaker kept outside for the benefit of those who aren't committed enough to get in and squat on the floor through two and a half hours of concert music. But, for the 200-odd listeners who manage to squeeze in within handshaking distance of the musicians, it is raw, mike-less music undistorted by the amplifier. You are free from the musical electrocution that goes on in the regular south Indian concert halls with their indifferent acoustics and screeching sound systems. This music chamber is no transit lounge for listeners to freely stroll in and out as the performance is in progress and make even more noise than the musicians. Nothing of the kind is permitted here, not even the customary applauding.

In the absence of an overbearing and easily distracted audience, the musicians relax and focus. And you come away with no-nonsense music at its best.

However austere and low profile, this series of Navaratri concerts in Thiruvananthapuram is a

Left and bottom:
Navaratri Mandapam, Thiruvananthapuram.
For a stretch of nine evenings in a year this
little chamber provides quality Karnatak
music undistorted by amplification.

Kuthiramalika, Thiruvananthapuram.
This palace of Travancore's erstwhile
ruling family is a favoured venue
for open-air music concerts.

Hindustani classical musician Saratchandra Raghunath Marathe and wife Manisha in their rented bedsitter in Kozhikode.

set, institutionalised tradition. But it is left to hapless individuals to sustain certain other streams of music Kerala has played host to. Saratchandra Raghunath Marathe teaches Hindustani classical music in Kozhikode. He came here as a 20-year-old in 1953. Through 48 years, from one run-down rented house to the next, the music has stayed. So has the poise of the childless couple. Marathe and wife Manisha smile a lot when one of their "hundred children" calls on them. One such disciple is the 49-year-old Balakrishnan, who works at a jewellery shop and takes time off to learn the flute.

In Kuttichira, a suburb of Kozhikode, music surfaces when night falls. Ordinary-looking men earn their uncertain incomes by the day and sing their hearts out by night. You go up a stairway that can't get steeper to find a singing fraternity in darkness. The power has been cut off but the club's devoted members sit down in candlelight to chat and tune up. In the flickering light you float like a space tourist. Perched precariously atop a row of shops, the low-roofed little room has crumbling walls that carry portraits of local legends like the late Baburaj. The building seems to be held together by musical notes.

A couple of lanes away, you find yourself on firmer ground but amidst the stormy temper of Abdul Razak. This *sufi* singer rants at his young percussionist friend Hari for having brought

visitors without notice. Razak cools down soon enough to sing like a pro.

On your own you won't get far in Kochi's maze of melodies. You need local help from the likes of Nelson, a trade unionist and a lyricist in his own right and M. Iqbal, who works for a bank and chronicles local culture. They conduct you through cheek-by-jowl tenements and you cross the living space of numerous amused families to find music. In a spotlessly clean 10-square-feet shack overlooking the Calvetti Bridge, the grandmotherly Khaulathu Itha sits on the edge of her cot and sings a Muslim folk-song with the lilt of a teenager.

V.M. Charles forgets he is 80 and leaps up to his full six feet to demonstrate Chavittu Natakam, a hybrid dance-drama Kochi culled out of Portuguese and local theatre arts. The diminutive Khalid lives on a dollar a day and when he isn't selling fish he sings Urdu *ghazals* with a flair and diction that do not come easily to a south Indian. Mehboob is all over the place. People stop you to point out a footbridge the late musician walked across and a street lamp he sat under to sing their favourite songs. If music can give you such posthumous presence, you don't need religion.

Why haven't such bursts of micro-music added up? In matters musical Kerala seems frozen in a sedentary time warp. Quite like the land itself divided by 44 rivers into stamp-sized domains

The little Khalid of Fort Kochi. Sings Urdu *ghazals* with a flair unheard in these parts.

A private concert by Abdul Razak,
the *sufi* singer, in his house in Kuttichira,
Kozhikode, with Hari on the tabla.

Khaulathu Itha, the evergreen exponent
of Muslim folk melodies.

Simhanada Bhagawati Temple without an idol in Tharakkad, Palakkad. Locals treat it as a routine place of worship little knowing that it is a unique shrine for sound (*nada*).

with enough water to sustain life and localise culture. Is it taboo for music as it has been for much else in the pre-modern times to cross the waters? Neither trade winds nor more recently the airwaves helped. The state-run radio was well received here but it had other priorities. The mercantile culture didn't spin off much music either.

Thanks to overseas trade, thriving bazaars must surely have showcased wares on this coast on the lines of the Saint Bartholomew Fair. From 1133 to 1855 this trade fair remained a popular business event in Smith-field, London and became a great place for music. Over the years it entertained visitors with "Musick booths" for ensemble music to ballad operas. In the 18th century, it hosted *The Beggar's Opera*, the low-life theatre that parodied the gentlefolk's Italian opera. With all its subaltern pretensions, Kerala never produced protest music on this scale. What little local micro-music there is with or without defiant undertones is trailing off. Can't sight new takers.

Cacofonix dominates the Kerala soundtrack with more noise than music. And there is not even a Neil Diamond here to rhapsodise about the "beautiful noise coming out from the streets ..." ◆

V.M. Charles. This well-known performer of
Chavittu Natakam, a hybrid dance-drama
culled out of Portuguese and local
theatre arts, is now retired and in
his '80s, but can give you a
vigorous 10-minute demo.

BEYOND WHAT YOU SEE AND HEAR

The Druid

Asterix conducted you through the sights and Cacofonix through the sounds of Kerala. Now it is the turn of Getafix the druid to take you beyond on a more mysterious journey. Sixty plus, bespectacled and fidgeting with his little box of chewing tobacco, the druid was lounging in the unlikeliest of places. Kattumadam Narayanan Namboodiri sat chatting in the Banerjee Club at Thrissur. He is no longer as keen a club-goer as he used to be in his pre-druid days when he ran a business and espoused Left radical views. This unique combination of commerce and communism came naturally to Kerala's landed gentry as the state was turning red in the 1950s. Since then Kattumadam has grown out of both to take up familial responsibility as the patriarch of the paranormal – a role he lately delegated to his son.

He calls you home to witness an annual family offering to the *chathans* – described a bit unfairly as "demons" by Dr Hermann Gundert, the first major lexicographer in Malayalam. You'll see as you go along that they aren't that evil but they certainly are spirits with occult powers. If you expect to drive into an eerie setting in the middle of nowhere, you'll be disappointed. There is nothing to tell this riveraine countryside apart. Kattumadam lives in a typical small-townish Kerala village.

The evening's ceremonies are to take place in his house, over 200 years old with exposed walls of 20-inch-thick laterite. It is a pruned version of his ancestral house. Which was some 28,000 square feet of built-up area. To run such stadium-scale residential units, it takes a retinue of retainers and hangers-on, which only a feudal society can supply.

Feudal landholding is a thing of the past but what has stayed intact is the family's magical legacy. The band of *chathans* is still loyal to the Kattumadam household. These netherworldly imps must have been lurking in the lengthening shadows, visible to their master but beyond your sinful eyes and mine. Kattumadam has had his sinful days too, his old friends will tell you. He was fond of the good things of life including the most mind-bending of all – books.

The young Brahmin made up for his erratic schooling by reading his way into the heady eclectic progressive mindset that went by the name of Marxism in the then Kerala. In the bargain, he must have transited feudal decline quite painlessly. Eventually he seems to have lived down his left-wing past too without the typical withdrawal symptoms of the ranting former communist. Above all, he spares you the overzealous afterthoughts of the born-again believer.

Reclining in his armchair in the sit-out of his outhouse, he casually checks on the arrangements for the evening. With a half smile that never leaves his face, the lord and master of

The 200-year-old ancestral house of the Kattumadam family.

Kattumadam Narayanan Namboodiri,
the lord and master of the *chathans*.

the *chathans* is slowly preparing to receive his ethereal subjects. And you wait around for the celebrations to begin in the tantalising hope that some Shakespearean manifestation of Prospero's Ariel will appear.

What follows is a line-up of ritual arts. Three men are taking their time over a six-foot-long five-colour image of Vettaikkorumakan, a hunting god who got duly appropriated into the Hindu pantheon as a presence of Shiva. The stylised form takes shape as programmed hands sprinkle coloured powder on the floor – the way pixel after pixel would appear on a super-slow computer screen. After this visual slow motion comes the breathtaking audio – *tayambaka*. This percussion ensemble spirals its way through Kerala's very own intricate rhythmic scales to reach an electrifying crescendo. You can't ask for more "atmosphere". By now night has fallen and it belongs to the *velichapad* – variously described as "the temple oracle" and "the divine dancer". His role here is choreographic. He is ceremoniously ushered into the house to the accompaniment of drums and pipes. There, he dances around and eventually into the powder spread of the tribal icon on the floor to finally erase most of it. Festivities conclude with the breaking of 108 coconuts – a fraction of the 12,000 that was customary in grander times.

You come away with no spooky high. Which is the last thing Kattumadam promises in the first

place. He wouldn't cash in on your fear. He likes to use the esoteric if at all medically – to help people overcome mental blocks. He is a benevolent patron to his subtle imps who seem more like playful pranksters than scary monsters. The sort who at worst stone your house and break a tile here and a windowpane there to unsettle you a bit before vanishing into the night without a trace.

The unseen spiritual serfs elsewhere are an overworked lot. They have to sweat it out to generate public fear and private finance for their masters. There are Mercedes- and BMW-owning families in the Peringottukara town whose entire economy is run by the *chathans*. Home-based establishments woo customers most competitively. All along the highway, signboard after signboard proclaims extra authentic links with the spirits. One is reminded of an old *Punch* cartoon, which shows a picket line of ghosts challenging a rival union over the right to haunt a house.

There are "genuine" *chathans*, "real" *chathans* and "original" *chathans*. You can choose between brands to alleviate your darkest dread and fulfil your most secret wish. The closely held and selectively leaked-out client list extends from insecure politicians to ambitious poets. While such focused commercial activity on the extra-sensory is confined to certain pockets, Kerala as a whole has been traditionally home to magical beings of all sizes and shapes.

Toddy tapper Vijayan in R Block, Kuttanad. The high in Kerala is right up there for you to tap – the toddy from the swaying palm trees.

The image of Vettaikkorumakan, the hunting tribal god, being laid out on the floor.

The drinking deity Muthappan
in Parassinikadavu.

Velichapad, the divine dancer,
warming up for the concluding
ceremony of the evening at
Kattumadam's house;
The velichappad dances around
and eventually into the five-colour
image of the tribal deity on
the floor and erases most of it.

Theories abound on why. Sample the following:

It is all very well to rave about the lush green paradise that Kerala is. But if you live day in and day out in a heaven on earth it could get pretty tiresome. The Malayali gets easily bored with the real and looks around to maintain his high. Which in the potable form is pretty easy to find in this land of "kera", the coconut (and hence "Kerala-m"). Palm liquor fermented or distilled is the basic magic potion that has long depressed native inhibitions. Spirit of one kind complements another. Even the gods don't abstain. The colourfully masked tribal deities in Parassinikadavu have made a morning ritual of imbibing in grand style amidst thunderous drumming and drunken dancing. Keralites however don't need any divine persuasion to tipple. Today they constitute the hardest drinking community in the country.

Yet another view is that people here have always had too much leisure on their hands. Even those who were no more than slaves. Given the apartheid-grade social discrimination that proscribed the upper-caste master from coming within telescopic distance of the outcaste and the lower-caste toiler, the farm hands could have found ways to skulk, shirk and daydream. The proverbially idling mind can surely think up a thing or two. Conversely, from the high-caste end, the sun-tanned serfs might well have been seen as a distant blur on the horizon. This is the kind of lordly gaze that cre-

ates the likes of chathans, the potentially defiant serfs whose defiance is transposed to a magical world over which the master retains ultimate control.

You can reel off more theories but can't explain away Kerala's considerable ageless ghostly population. Which has survived a much-hyped spell of atheistic Marxism. Non-believers have now turned into closet-believers. Popular writers, those unerring weathercocks, are on an overdrive to conjure up scary characters. Black magic and exorcism have for a while been part of best-selling pulp fiction. The latest to be haunted is the TV set. When prime-time ghosts are having a free run in the living room, one can only assume that Kerala's family audiences are a blissfully uninhibited lot.

Maybe one last attempt at making sense of the Malayali is in order. His mind has been repeatedly engraved and re-engraved with not much effacing done in between. On our quest, every theoriser from the social scientist to the pop-sociologist has fallen by the wayside. So let us turn to the astrologer. He will tell you that the Malayali's horoscope has an extra variable – a shadow planet called gulikan. Who is a potent spoiler to boot. Makes matters a lot less predictable in these parts. Should inspire the kind of uncertain story-line that will make a comic book sparkle. There is a little Asterix, a louder Cacofonix and a laid-back druid waiting here for an author. ◆

INDEX

Page number in italics refer to captions of sketches